CO 1 54 843

BCAS
BARNARD CASTLE

7/97

BP. AUCKLAND

22.5.98

CLS

A 22.2.99

17. FEB. 1999

PETE

− 4 JAN 2008

lc

5484338

BOOKSTORE LOAN

Please return/renew this item by the last date shown

DURHAM COUNTY COUNCIL
ARTS, LIBRARIES AND MUSEUMS

The Marriage Service

David Male

Hodder & Stoughton

LONDON SYDNEY AUCKLAND

Copyright © 1996 by David Male.

First published in Great Britain 1996.

The right of David Male to be identified as the author of the work
has been asserted by him in accordance with the
Copyright, Designs and Patents Act 1988.

Unless otherwise indicated Scripture quotations are taken from
the HOLY BIBLE, NEW INTERNATIONAL VERSION.
Copyright © 1973, 1978, 1984 by International Bible Society.
Used by permission of Hodder and Stoughton Ltd.
All rights reserved.

Extracts from *The Book of Common Prayer*, the rights of which are
vested in the Crown, are reproduced by permission of the Crown's
Patentee, Cambridge University Press.

The Alternative Service Book 1980 is copyright © The Central Board
of Finance of the Church of England. Extracts are reproduced with
permission.

10 9 8 7 6 5 4 3 2 1

All rights reserved.
No part of this publication may be reproduced, stored in a retrieval
system, or transmitted, in any form or by any means
without the prior written permission of the publisher,
nor be otherwise circulated in any form of binding or cover
other than that in which it is published and without a similar condition
being imposed on the subsequent purchaser.

British Library Cataloguing in Publication Data
A record for this book is available from the British Library.

ISBN 0 340 64199 1

Designed and typeset by Kenneth Burnley at Typograph,
Irby, Wirral, Cheshire.
Printed and bound in Great Britain by Cox & Wyman Ltd,
Reading, Berkshire.

Hodder and Stoughton Ltd
A division of Hodder Headline PLC
338 Euston Road
London NW1 3BH

Contents

	Foreword *by the Bishop of Wakefield*	7
1	Why get married in church?	9
2	Where do I stand?	19
3	Where does God fit in on the day?	29
4	What is happening to us at the wedding?	43
5	What do we promise?	53
6	Is that the end, or just the beginning?	65
	Appendix 1: Suggested readings	71
	Appendix 2: Popular wedding hymns	73
	Appendix 3: Any questions?	75

# Foreword
by the Bishop of Wakefield

AT A TIME WHEN THERE is much discussion about marriage, it is enormously helpful to have this clear and positive treatment of the marriage service. David Male writes from his experience as a sensitive pastor who is fully aware of the pressures which modern society imposes on the total commitment required of those who make their marriage vows.

There is in these pages much encouragement and wise guidance. Against the current background of depressingly high numbers of divorces, David Male's positive approach shows that marriage is a wonderful gift from God. When properly prepared for and continually worked at, marriage provides great blessings and the capacity to face together every joy and sorrow.

The Church of England 'affirms, according to our Lord's teaching, that marriage is in its nature a union permanent and life-long, for better, for worse, till death them do part, of one man with one woman, to the exclusion of all others on either side' (Canon B30).

It is my prayer that this book will help many couples to make that vision become for them a lifelong reality – and a source, therefore, of enormous blessing and lasting happiness.

✠ *Nigel Wakefield*
January 1996

CHAPTER 1

 Why get married in church?

THE WHOLE OF YOUR LIFE changed in the most dramatic and vivid way in a mere 45 minutes? Surely not. Such a big change in such a short time. Is it possible? A wedding offers that possibility for it alters your legal status and recasts your social position in the community. People treat you differently from now on. You may find it requires you to go as far as changing your name. You find yourself saying in public the most intimate of statements, things that normally you would not say in front of your closest friend. Your heart is laid open to public scrutiny. It necessarily involves your spiritual and emotional resources being tapped and your bank balance may suffer! All this takes place in the company of those who are closest and dearest to you, many having made long trips just to be part of these 45 minutes. They want desperately to be with you and to encourage you in this dramatic and all-consuming change.

This change is immense in its proportions. You can never, never be the same person or have the same state. Outlook, lifestyle, priorities, choice, finances, and future are now up for grabs. Nothing can be taken for granted, everything is now renegotiable. Far more hangs on this short time than seems possible. It is the focus of the most important decision of your life. Its far-reaching impact is immeasurable, its possibilities endless and its joys boundless.

Surprisingly this radical change can be achieved fairly simply. It doesn't even necessarily involve moving from where you live. The arrangements can vary from the most simple to something that requires military-style planning and precision. The cost can be limiting or limitless. It may involve five people or five thousand and it requires no special skills, protracted negotiations or sophisticated pyrotechnics. All is achieved by the simplest of ceremonies. It just needs a sprinkling of well-chosen, traditional words, some of which are repeated by those in attendance. These few plain words, though, cannot mask the enormity of the occasion on the lives of those taking part.

In essence a church wedding is a most simple ceremony, yet it is a chameleon of an event, changing its colours to fit in with its surroundings. But it remains steadfastly a wedding service. The service can at one level be seen as involving just a local church, a minister, a couple intending to pronounce their love for each other and their supporters. Yet while retaining the essentials, it can become a national spectacle, resplendent with cathedral, a bishop, a congregation of the nation's notables and an estimated TV audience of 100 million people.

Whatever hue the ceremony takes, the plain fact is that the service is one of the most profound, influential and deep moments of anyone's life. Kerry Mansfield of Relate commented in a newspaper article 'Most people would never enter a marriage if they didn't think there was something mystical in it.' For the couple, the life-changing significance of this event is exciting and exhilarating, while at the same time awesome and even terrifying. In a few short moments everything changes. Singleness and all its attractions will cease. There is now a partner to think about and a new life together to consider. Finances and the future to be shared. Plans have to be constructed, priorities worked out, a house turned into a home, a monotony of household chores allocated and there is always the reception! No wonder the wedding ceremony says that marriage is not something to be entered into lightly or carelessly!

Someone soon to be married commented in an article on marriage in the *Independent* newspaper 'I want to marry with the maximum ritual, pomp and ceremony. You want to make it the most awe-inspiring and overwhelming event you can, with all the weight of history and tradition and a sense of cosmic significance.

WHY GET MARRIED IN CHURCH?

It is probably the most important thing you will ever do, except, perhaps, giving birth or dying, so it is worth thinking about, planning and getting ready for.' To enter into such a vital time with little thought or consideration would be foolhardy. Effort spent in preparation for this event cannot be wasted. But preparation is not purely limited to the consideration of clothes, food and venue. As well as the material element of the day, it involves the emotional and spiritual aspects. For above all, the wedding centres on our emotional and spiritual lives as two people come together to start a new life as one.

For anyone considering a church wedding and maybe wondering whether or not it is for them, it is encouraging to remember that such ceremonies have happened the length and breadth of this land for hundreds of years. Many thousands have found such a service to be the best way to start this life-changing partnership. To choose a church wedding is to continue a long, long line of people who have discovered in this ceremony something that meets their deepest needs and longings. Church weddings are still the most popular method for getting married. For example in 1991 there were over 300,000 church weddings in Great Britain. The history and the numbers suggest that a church wedding works well for many people.

So why has this practice continued successfully? Why do so many people consider a similar event for themselves? Perhaps you are thinking about a church wedding for yourself or a relative. It must be admitted that a church wedding is not the only option. Many people now choose a civil ceremony in a Registry Office. They want to commit themselves to each other publicly and legally but they do not want to do this within a religious framework. In this ceremony, in the presence of a registrar, relatives and friends they will make promises to each other and complete the necessary paperwork. Recently the choice was widened further. Now couples are able to hold such a non-religious ceremony in a building other than a Registry Office, as long as it has been approved for marriage by the local authority. This does not allow for weddings in the open air or a marquee, but only in buildings which observe the dignity of the occasion. Stately homes and hotels are the sort of buildings deemed suitable. Other couples decide to commit themselves to each other exclusively but see no need to do this within a religious or even a secular framework. For them it's not a piece of paper that is important but their intentions towards each other.

A church wedding is undoubtedly a wonderful and a momentous occasion. But questions need to be asked and issues faced as decisions are made. What might be good and positive reasons for wanting to have a wedding service in church, even if the people are not regular churchgoers?

It's easy to be caught up in the world of childhood dreams or in the glitzy presentation of show business weddings in glossy magazines. Many young girls dream of the day when, like Cinderella, they marry their handsome prince. My four-year-old daughter has already been through countless wedding services in her play. She has married everything from her sister to the cat! Beautiful flowing white dresses, a multitude of bridesmaids, a quaint and ancient church are some of the ingredients of this dream-like image. A *Daily Express* article about how brides choose their wedding dress quoted a mum as saying, 'Stephanie has always been romantic. She has always fantasised about this.' In this dream world the day is seen from the viewpoint of the bride. This is often carried over into the real event with the day being referred to as the 'bride's day'. For many brides, wonderful dreams do become a reality. A church can provide the ideal setting for the image of a perfect wedding day. The possibilities for fulfilling hopes and aspirations can be wonderfully met, and rightly so. A leading article in a newspaper described a church wedding as 'aesthetic, solemn, beautiful and traditional with an overall sense of event'. Not a bad description is it?

Hopefully, though, there is more to the ceremony than the undoubted theatre of the occasion. One of the wonders of the church service is that it takes us to a deeper level. It goes far beyond the surface level of clothes, looks, impressions and fashion. It takes us 'Back to Basics', to our core values, to the things that make us truly human. It touches far more than the surface issues of what we can see or hear or touch. It brings us face to face with those things that are the heartbeat of our human existence. We come to the essential world of love, commitment, choice, support, care and togetherness. In an article on marriage in the *Independent*, a bride-to-be commented that 'a religious ceremony gives you the time and the symbols to lay full value on what you are doing, to enjoy the moment and to make the commitment'. Are those the kind of things you want to think about at such a time? Do you want to share these values? Do you want to celebrate these virtues? Then a church wedding is not a bad place to begin or continue this search.

Like emerging rivers, we human beings often search for the line of least resistance. We can become masters of searching for the easy way, that path that will cause least fuss or aggravation. Sometimes we exhibit this on a very mundane level. In conversation we often agree with whatever is said because we can't be bothered or are too fearful to disagree. We often yearn for the easy life, to be left in peace to enjoy ourselves, whatever compromises we have to make to attain this position.

Unfortunately this can be a particularly dangerous way of living when it comes to weddings. It's all too easy to opt for a church wedding simply to please somebody else. It's so much easier to keep quiet and to keep your head down than to muddy the waters. There can be pressure on one or both partners from parents, social expectations or even each other. It may seem easier to silently back down and keep your opinions to yourself. Yet I would suggest that such a peace-keeping formula may be a false economy. It is vital that both partners feel not only comfortable with what is going to happen on their wedding day but also that this is what they want for themselves as well as the other person. The pressures may seem unbearable but this is too important a moment in your lives just to acquiesce to the demands placed on you.

It is important that the couple sit down together and talk honestly and openly about what they want. There is nothing worse than one of them, on this wonderful wedding day, secretly wishing they were somewhere else or going about it in some other way. They need together to decide that this is what they want to do and to discuss why they want to do it. On such a wonderful occasion it's good to know that you both want this and that you are both committed to making it the best day it can possibly be.

Luck and fate seem to play a large part in the lives of many people. We may be sophisticated, scientific, computer-literate people but many of us still touch wood, throw salt or avoid a workman's ladder. This kind of thinking can also subtly find its way into considering whether to have a church wedding. A church wedding is seen by many people I meet as a guarantee to a lucky start. Now, we are all concerned to have the best beginning for a couple who are getting married. But is it a good idea to look upon the church as a talisman, ensuring good luck, health and a favourable future? Can some simple words spoken in a religious building act as a kind of a 'spiritual rabbit's foot'?

Of course a wedding service in church is a good place to begin married life but this has more to do with the content of the service than any lucky vibes of the building. Occasionally brides have refused to walk a certain way into the church in which I work because it is deemed as being unlucky. Sometimes I see the services of a chimney sweep being employed so that the couple can be photographed alongside him in order to encourage good luck in the months and years that lie ahead. Such quaint old customs are often part of our social heritage but the wedding service itself suggests that a successful marriage needs a stronger foundation than good fortune or lady luck. We need resources that are more trustworthy, more reliable and much more powerful than a chimney sweep can provide. The service itself continually tries to point us to resources that do not rely on such random factors as being in the right place at the right time or doing certain things in particular ways.

What if a couple want a church wedding but feel there may be too many obstacles to overcome? Sometimes people who would like a church wedding for the best of motives are put off for reasons that may not be insurmountable. They may have worries or fears about the ceremony which may, with a little effort, be easily overcome. One of the main inhibitors is finance. In a recent survey of women 25 per cent said the thing that may stop them from getting married is the cost. If you believe many of today's glossy magazines, you cannot achieve a meaningful day and expect any change from £5,000. I recently read a newspaper report which suggested that the average wedding cost more than £8,500! The article then went on to suggest that with such high sums being spent, insurance cover against misfortune on the day may be a wise precaution. Unfortunately the cover does not include the partner failing to appear but would pay out for a forgetful photographer, heavy snow or an exploding bottle of champagne. *Brides* magazine estimates that a church wedding, with a marquee reception and 150 guests would set you back between £8,000 and £15,000 though I doubt any wedding would come close to the estimated £22 million spent on a wedding in Dubai! There were 20,000 guests seated in a specially built stadium and the celebrations extended over seventeen days. Or what about the £1 million Elizabeth Taylor spent on her ninth wedding ceremony?

Such costs seem frightening. You may be contemplating buying a house or its contents and find the outlay of a wedding to be completely out of the question for you and your family. Or you may just not have anything like that kind of money. Don't worry: most churches cost a fraction of this. Not all the additions are essential to make the day meaningful for you and for others. If you want simplicity or are under financial constraints, a church service is not out of the question. The day can be kept simple, without losing the depth, joy and celebration of what you are doing. The outlay for the church service itself is fairly minimal. It is usually the other accessories which make the final cost so high. One vicar in Manchester was so upset by the escalating cost of weddings that he publicised cut-price weddings. This included organising the reception flowers and even the honeymoon!

Sometimes couples can be put off by the church itself. Without meaning to, it can easily give the impression of a religious club which is skilfully run to satisfy those who attend and to repel those who do not. Sometimes churches can seem more like impregnable castles than welcoming places where you can join others in finding the living God. The castle, with total efficiency, protects those who are sheltering from the ravages of real life, while successfully keeping everyone else and reality away from those who are safe within its walls. Yet if the church is to fulfil the charter which its founder originally gave, then it should be a very different place. Defences need to come down, for it was founded to be a place with open doors and a warm welcome.

Couples who are already living together but now want to have a wedding service in church may feel that their decision to live together has forfeited their right to a church wedding. Usually this is not the case but it is worth talking it over with the minister and thinking about the wedding's implications.

The good news is that most ministers are very happy to talk with people as they explore the possibility of a church wedding. They are happy to talk not only about the practical and legal details and arrangements but also the vital issues that lie at the heart of the service. They want to help people explore the amazing richness of the service so that they can receive the full benefits of the day. It then becomes much more than a jumble of religious words. It is important that couples understand what is happening, for as we have seen its implication are massive. This one day will affect all the other days of the couple's life. I would urge any couple thinking about a wedding to get in touch with a local church minister as soon as they can. Other people may be able to offer very useful advice but the minister will be able to tell you what is required, available and possible.

Many of the issues which I have touched upon are powerful forces in shaping our decisions, some of them rightly so. The danger is that they can force couples to do something that they are not totally happy with. It is vital, for their own integrity and enjoyment, that they are comfortable with what is decided upon and planned for. Ultimately this is not a decision for parents, friends or relatives but the couple themselves. Such a day is too important in anybody's life for them to be railroaded into it. It is vital that a couple talks about the wedding day and what they want and most importantly why they want it. Relationships are all about communication, something which is needed as they talk over how and why they are to start this new life together.

So does a church service offer something that civil ceremonies cannot? Does it possess a quality or element that cannot be found in any other place? Are there positive reasons for choosing a church service other than just 'It's a nice thing to do'? Is *Brides* magazine right when it commented recently that couples are going back to traditional marriage?

I often hear those who have got married or those in congregations at weddings support the idea that a church wedding does provide something extra. They may not have been in church for years but they express it in such ways as 'There is something special about being in church', 'It gives the whole day a different atmosphere' or 'You can't beat a church wedding'. I think these people are trying to express more than the feeling that it's a quaint building, ideal for photos or 'the place to be'. They are trying to put into words their feelings that there is an extra dimension. The church provides a reminder that, as the couple stand in front of their family and friends, and make promises to each other, there is more to our lives and our love than is immediately observable. A church wedding links us firmly to this part of our lives which is commonly called the 'spiritual'. The problem is often that this word can be off-putting for many people. It conjures up images of nuns and monks, or a kind of other-worldly escapism. Yet it is only a reminder that there is someone beyond us and bigger than us. The good news that the Christian faith proclaims is that God is not aloof, ineffectual or powerless but that he wants to be involved in every aspect of our lives, not least our wedding day and marriage. I am not suggesting that a successful marriage is impossible without a Christian commitment but many who have discovered that God is alive and real would say that bringing his love into the centre of their lives gives them the best possible start and the most powerful helper. It is easy for us to think that the wedding service is simply the prelude to the real business of the day, the reception. Of course the reception is a wonderful event and needs plenty of planning and organisation. I hope though, as couples realise what they are saying and before whom they are making these promises, that they will want to put as much effort into the planning of the service as the reception.

The wedding service itself can be a nerve-racking time for many couples as they stand alone before the assembled congregation. They can feel vulnerable as they realise the wonderful enormity of what the day means. They are on the threshold of a new relationship which they hope will develop and deepen for the rest of their lives together. The future can seem both exciting and challenging but also daunting and dangerous. The service can act as a tremendous reminder that someone far stronger than us, more reliable , more resourceful and dependable than us wants to stand with the couple on their wedding day and every day after that.

Your own belief in God may be simple, confused, hazy or casual. You may not know what you think about God. The wedding service may even be able to help with that. The great news about a church wedding is that it offers the possibility of 'touching base' with the One who made you, loves you and offers himself for you. If this claim is true, as many have found it to be, it's not a bad place for a couple to start the most important relationship of their entire existence, is it?

CHAPTER 2

Where do I stand?

I LOVE WATCHING PEOPLE. It's fascinating, as people go about their daily business, to see how they react to other people and situations they encounter. I am fortunate in that my study is on the third storey of our house and overlooks a park. Often when I should be working I gaze out of the window and study people walking their dogs, talking with their friends or just taking a leisurely stroll. On a train many of us enjoy studying other people. From what they are doing, how they look and how they act we try to guess what job they do or what kind of person they may be. This whole process has been given scientific backing by books like Desmond Morris's *Man Watching* which was also made into a successful TV series. The experts tell us that we communicate as much with our body as with our words. If that surprises you watch two people in conversation and see how they use their bodies to help them in getting their point across. Compare the body language of a couple deeply in love talking gently to each other and then two people having a heated argument. You will quickly notice how differently they use their bodies in communicating. Or you can do such a study on yourself and note your body position in different places and with different people. It all happens subconsciously but it does express a lot of our true feelings about a person or situation.

You might be wondering what this social analysis has to do with the wedding service. The answer is that it's not just words that are important in the service but bodies as well. The wedding service uses the fact that our bodies as well as our words communicate what we want to express. The wedding service uses the bodies of the principal characters as a moving commentary on the service. The service has a dramatic quality as those involved act out the deep meaning of what is taking place. It's not a static tableau but a dynamic event full of colour, movement and drama. The wedding service is like a stage play. It is important to know not only what you say but where you say it from.

Many couples instinctively see this movement as vitally important. There is one question that I am nearly always asked by a couple when I talk with them in the church at the rehearsal. It is not about the form of service, the music or the photos but simply 'Where do we stand?' This seems to be the problem that wakes them up in the middle of the night in a cold sweat. 'When it comes to the vows, where should we be?' Quite often on the wedding day itself, as I leave the bridegroom sitting on the front pew the last words he utters to me are, 'Now where do I stand again when she comes in?'

So let's look at the question of where the principal characters stand and how they are moved around in the service. But why don't we also do a bit of people-watching and try and decide from these movements what they are trying to communicate.

'And they are under starter's orders.' These words are often used at the beginning of a horse-racing commentary. For example at the beginning of the Grand National the horses are led to the start of the race. They then line up but are prevented from starting by a large white tape. This tape is then lifted as the starter begins the race. As we begin thinking about the service we need to go to the start and think about how the main participants begin to get ready for the service.

Obviously, precise answers to 'Where do I stand?' vary with local practice, the geography of the building and the particular denominational service. Despite these variations most services follow a basic pattern. The service begins with the congregation seated in the church awaiting the bride's arrival. The bridegroom and best man (or woman) wait anxiously, usually in the front pew on the right-hand side of the church. At this point, members of the congregation are continually turning towards the main door of the church to see if the bride has arrived yet. This is the moment when even the most confident bridegroom feels the blood rushing towards his feet and blind panic slowly setting in.

The action then really begins as the bride arrives at the church. She does not come alone. There is an escort of her father (or whoever is going to give her away) plus bridesmaids and perhaps pageboys. Often a photographer will take a few shots at the church door. The church minister meets them at the church door and arranges them for that initial walk down the aisle. The bride is at the front of the line accompanied at the left side by whoever is giving her away. The bridesmaids and pageboys, usually arranged in twos, follow on behind.

This ordering of those involved is not arbitrary. It is done to communicate that this is the end of the old and the beginning of the new. As the organist plays some suitable music the bride, often veiled, walks serenely down the aisle with her escorts. Her escorts, as family and friends, represent her life up till now, her life before today. But something new and wonderful is about to begin. A new order and new relationships are going to be established in the next few moments that are intended to last a lifetime.

The line up
This short walk down the aisle puts the bride centre-stage. Everyone is desperate to get a look at her dress and admire her bridesmaids. It is also the preliminary to the start of the service itself. Now where they stand at the front of the church says a lot about what is happening. It will not just be words that play an important role but their position and body posture. As the bride approaches, the bridegroom moves out from his pew to stand centre-stage at the front. The bride takes her place on the left of her husband-to-be. At this point they face not each other, but the minister to whom their initial words will be addressed. They are flanked by their escorts. On the extreme right side stands the best man (usually) and on the extreme left the bride's father. Depending on the room available the bridesmaids and pageboys stand behind the couple. The couple are surrounded by those who are

close to them but these are not the centre of attention. The emerging new order now has the couple firmly at the centre of proceedings. It is often now that the bridesmaids help the bride to take her veil back so that she is prepared to marry her intended.

The start

The order of the service can vary considerably at the beginning. Often the minister welcomes everyone, a hymn is sung, followed by the marriage part of the service. Sometimes a reading and even a short talk might precede this. In the Methodist church there are three different options for the order of the service. So it is worth talking with the minister about what is usually done in a particular church. The couple may be able to have some choice in this. A basic pattern for the service after the welcome and opening hymn may be:

> Introduction to what marriage is, why get married and its responsibilities.
> Question about legal impediments.
> Consent of two individuals.
> Father's agreement.
> Vows.
> Exchange of rings.
> Declaration of marriage
> Blessing.

This is then followed by one or two readings from the Bible, a sermon, prayers, a hymn, the signing of the registers and the final blessing or a mixture of some of the above. But I stress this is only a possible order.

Most Christian denominations have their own form of marriage service. They usually follow the same basic form with some changes in order or wording. If a couple are getting married in the Church of England they usually have a choice of two forms of service. There is the older traditional service from the *Book of Common Prayer* (1662) or the *Alternative Service Book* (1980). (For the rest of the book these will be referred to as *BCP* and *ASB*). The modern service (*ASB*) is probably the more popular one these days. The only main differences are in the language, and at a few points there is a different order or emphasis. In this book we will generally be following the service in the more modern *ASB* service. A couple might want to look at both services and see what they think. It is worth thinking about which words are most easily understood by the couple and by the congregation. There is little sense in going through a service which is hard to follow.

As the marriage service begins the minister explains to the couple and the congregation what the marriage is about, its importance, seriousness and God's role in it. This information is obviously not new to the couple but serves as a reminder of what an important event is about to take place. It emphasises that this is happening not only before those assembled at the church but before God.

Next the famous question about legal impediment is asked, first to the congregation and then to the couple. This question highlights the fact that this is a legal as well as a religious ceremony. For without the proper response (or more importantly the lack of response!) the ceremony cannot proceed. It often causes laughter and smiles as hopefully silence meets the words of the minister as he asks both the congregation and bride and groom whether the couple may lawfully marry. Certainly I often see relief on the faces of the bride and bridegroom as we go past this point. In the marriage services of quite a few other denominations, the couple are not asked a question but have to repeat a statement declaring that they know no legal impediment to the marriage.

A prospective mother-in-law shouting out that the girl is not good enough for her beloved son does not constitute a legal impediment to marriage! At a wedding in Nottingham which featured in many national papers, the groom's mother shouted at this point that her future daughter-in-law was a trollop and was not good enough for her boy! The only accusations that can stop the ceremony are (a) the claims that one of the partners is still legally married; or (b) that the couple are related to one another in one of the categories where marriage is forbidden (e.g. they are brother or sister); or (c) that one or both are under the legal age for marriage or are 16 or 17 but do not have parental consent. With such clear guidelines there is little chance of a serious interruption on the wedding day.

If a serious objection is made, the usual practice is for the minister, parents and couple plus anyone else involved to go to the vestry for the matter to be investigated. A clear case would have to be made for the minister to delay the wedding. He would then have to contact the Diocesan Registrar, who deals with the church's legal matters, as soon as possible. It is also usual for the objector to pay a sum of money as a bond in case the allegations are wrong or unfounded. But don't worry: such an eventuality is extremely rare.

The minister then asks the couple individually to state that they freely consent to the ceremony that is to take place. This is the first time that the couple are required to speak. This gives them quite a long time to relax from the beginning of the service before they have to say anything on their own. Each partner's answer is addressed not to each other but the minister. The answer of 'I will' looks back historically to the times of a public engagement ceremony when such a phrase was used. Now it shows that they give total consent to what is about to happen and that this consent involves a lifelong commitment. At a friend's wedding, a nervous groom remembering the first words he had to say was 'I will' unfortunately used these words when asked if there was any reason why they could not get married!

Next, the father is often asked 'Who gives this woman to be married?' or some similar words. In the newer Anglican service (*ASB*) this is optional and no specific words are given. This points to the idea of leaving the family for the first time and establishing a new family unit. In our society this is often not the case. The individuals may well have left home a long time before this service to set up independently of their family. This is an optional part of the service and certainly some couples feel it unhelpfully suggests that the bride is a piece of property to be passed from father to husband with little choice in the matter. But even today with our more mobile society it still proclaims something about a new order that is being established and that the couple are now responsible for each other.

Turn and face

The high point of the marriage service is now reached. The bride's father representing her life until now, returns to his seat in the congregation. The couple now make a subtle movement of their bodies which illustrates what is happening. They stop facing the minister and turn to face each other. You may wonder why this is important. It is saying that the vows they repeat are not vows made to the minister but to each other. As they say these promises they are marrying each other before God. The minister and the congregation, at this moment, act as witnesses to what is happening. The couple can either learn the vows and simply say them at the service, read them from a card or, as many prefer, repeat the vows as the minister quietly reads them. Again the communication is not by words alone. As each partner says their vows they take the other person's right hand. This was traditionally the way a legal and binding contract was entered into. It reminds everybody present that a lifelong, exclusive partnership is now emerging. This is intended to be no short-term contract.

The drama does not stop at this important moment. There are still two further symbolic acts which provide a dramatic commentary on the promises that have just been made. Firstly there is the symbolism of the rings. It is up to the couple whether both have a ring or just the bride. The ring acts as a physical reminder of the commitment that has just been entered into, it is to be like a badge which acts to tell others this person is married and to remind the wearer of the promises made. It reminds the couple that this relationship and the love contained within it is to be never-ending. The gold, of which the ring is made, is a sign of the value of this unique relationship. It is placed on the wearer's fourth finger on the left hand by the partner with some appropriate words.

The second symbolic act is performed by the minister. He first proclaims that after having made the vows they are now truly married. To symbolise this moment, he joins their right hands together (and in the *ASB* service) says 'that which God has joined together let no man divide', words of Jesus recorded in Matthew 19, verse 6. They show the importance God attaches to what has taken place. They are now joined together, a new relationship has begun and a new order started. Those last words also remind everybody present that there is even more going on than just words and movement. This has happened before the living God, and as the couple choose each other God sets his seal on this union and binds them together.

On your knees

In the Anglican service the couple are now invited to kneel. This is not just an opportunity to take the weight off their feet! It is a further part of the unfolding drama of the event. We are all familiar with the image of people being honoured by the Queen. As they receive the honour they kneel before her. This symbolises the recognition that they are in the presence of someone far greater and more powerful than themselves. In the same way as the couple kneel it is a recognition of who God is and that he has been part of all that has happened. The term for the prayer used is a 'blessing'. It means that God's protection, care and help are sought for the couple as they start their new life together. At the moment of their coming together, God is invited to be a part. After this, again, the service may vary. There is usually a hymn or two, a reading or readings from the Bible, a short talk and some prayers for the couple followed by a final blessing. It varies according to whether a couple sit or remain standing during the rest of the service. Local geography often dictates the answer to this. Then the registers, the records that confirm that the service has been legally and properly carried out, are signed by the couple, two witnesses and the minister. These two witnesses can be anybody from the congregation. Often they are the couple's relatives or closest friends. This can happen in the church itself, a side chapel or adjoining room. The best man, bridesmaids and parents are often in attendance for this.

Sometimes couples who are committed Christians take Communion towards the end of the service and occasionally Communion is available to anyone in the congregation who wants to partake. This was normal practice in the past but is much rarer these days. For some couples it is important that their first act together after marriage is to take Communion. This needs to be discussed carefully by the bride and groom together with the minister.

The finishing line

The end is now in sight as the couple, best man, bridesmaids and immediate family are lined up to process out of the church. The drama finishes through this final movement. The order of the line has changed from that at the beginning of the service. It is not now the bride and her father who lead the procession but the bride and groom. A new couple now walk out of church as husband and wife followed by their supporters. They walk back up the aisle to an appropriate piece of music. The new order of relationships has begun.

The wedding service is full of words but they are supplemented by these dramatic actions and movements. There have been meaningful entrances and departures and a liberal use of body language, including kneeling, facing each other and holding hands. There are significant changes in where people stand, in the giving of rings and much more. All the movements, the changing of participants and the postures combine to give this drama beauty and depth. It proclaims through words and actions that something new and marvellous has begun. Yet in this service the movement and words of one unseen guest pervades every aspect of what is taking place.

CHAPTER 3

Where does God fit in on the day?

IF YOU WERE PLANNING A WEDDING, how would you feel if someone turned up who was not on your meticulously prepared guest list? You have carefully organised family and friends, making sure with mathematical precision that the groom's and bride's families were equally represented. You argued over how to reduce the original list of 426 down to a manageable 108. What would you do? Maybe you would just ignore them, have them removed or enquire why they had turned up for your wedding? Whatever you did it might prove embarrassing. It's not a situation any of us would like to face.

But I can guarantee anyone considering a church wedding that there will be one guest at your day who is not on your list. You may wonder how I can be so certain about this fact. The reason is very simple. At every wedding I take, I publicly announce the fact that this guest is present. The first words of the (*ASB*) marriage service begin with, 'We have come together in the presence of God', or 'We are gathered here in the sight of God' in the older service (*BCP*). This guest may be unseen to all who are present but the living God promises to be at the service. Actually, it's not that he just turns up to join in with the celebrations, he is already there and we join with him on that special day. People's reactions to this may vary considerably, just as they would to a guest who was not on the guest list. They may be horrified, indignant, curious or just plain uninterested. So what can be done about this guest whose presence is proclaimed by the minister? What options are available?

Ignore him

This is perfectly possible. Unlike the baptism service, those participating in the marriage service are not asked to declare their own personal faith. They may approach the day with no belief in God or as one of his committed followers. They may feel that there is a God but any thoughts beyond that are hazy or confused. God can be sidelined in the service and on the day. That is not to say that the church service is unimportant but that any spiritual element might have minimal impact. Yet there is an increasing interest in spiritual things in Britain at the present time. A recent survey suggested that 66 per cent of the population feel that they belong to a religion while a newspaper editor recently described a church wedding as having enduring spirituality.

If your reaction to anything to do with God is to just ignore him as outdated, boring and irrelevant, I would ask you, before you approach the service, to give God a chance. You may know very little about him. You may be unable to see what relevance he has in your life or how he can have any impact on your relationship. Your experiences of churches and his followers may only confirm what you think. My first experiences produced in me a reaction of 'Forget it, this is a waste of time' but as I began to understand more I began to revise this initial diagnosis.

Before you write God off, let me ask you a simple question. What would be the best present a couple could receive on their wedding day? A house, a car, a washing machine . . . the list is endless. But what about a voucher that entitled them to gifts like love that they can rely on even when things go wrong, peace no matter what might be happening, the ability to encourage and build each other up rather than put each other down all the time. Patience even when they are being annoyed beyond what they can take, the ability to understand the other person's point of view. There are so many pressures on relationships. We are all aware of the many marriages that falter and fail. The Society of Wedding Photographers have had so much trouble with couples splitting up before they pay for their wedding album that they now require a divorce deposit, to protect themselves! There are pressures to have the right things, despite the ever-present danger for many of unemployment. Pressure from parents and families about the way they live their lives. Even pressure from each other to be the person the other wants you to be. It's very hard to live up to all these demands put upon a couple – from outside and from within their relationship. A psychiatrist recently commented that all the ideals of marriage can easily bring disillusionment.

I believe that, despite all the immediate attractions of a car or house, most of us ultimately want these material things only for what we feel they can give us, things like peace, happiness and joy. We would ultimately prefer to have the resources of love, peace, encouragement, patience and understanding because we know they are essential for a good relationship. These are the things that every relationship needs to have a long-term chance of success. We know that even these qualities do not give us 100 per cent guarantee for our relationship and its development – but they do give us a better chance of success. They are the things that will see us through the pressures and protect us from disillusionment.

The Christian faith and the service make a staggering claim which beats any sale offer that a shop can make. God wants, at no cost, to give these qualities and resources to every couple to enable them as people and as a couple to develop to their full potential. He desires the best for any and every marriage. The claim of the wedding service is that this is not just religious talk but that God can deliver! Is it not worth finding out whether he could do those things? Would it be better to give him a chance now or to ignore him and to find later that he could have made a difference?

Have him removed

After talking with people, including a church minister, you may be thinking about a Registry Office wedding. This wedding is a secular wedding and does not involve mentioning God. You may feel that is what you want. I am not saying that you stand no chance in your relationship without God; many couples have proved that not to be the case. But if God offers such benefits to us, is it not worth checking him out and seeing what he can come up with? Surely it's a risk worth taking, an offer that's worth considering?

Enquire why he is there

It may seem strange to suggest that we ask God some questions but that is what I would encourage you to do. You may well be asking how on earth can you ask God anything? You cannot see him and therefore it is easy to assume that he is not there or that he is a distant God who keeps the world going and does very little else. He is often portrayed as a heavenly grandpa, resplendent in his slippers and dressing gown but fading in his powers and presence. How can he be relevant to anyone today as they approach their wedding? The service itself provides an opportunity to ask questions of him and to begin to detect some answers to those vital issues. So let's give God a chance and allow him to answer our questions. We can then see what he has to say for himself.

What is God like?

'Ferndene School report on God. *Progress and Conduct:* I'm afraid that I'm severely disappointed in God's works. All three of him have shown no tendency to improve and he merely sits at the back of the class talking to himself. He has shown no interest in rugger, asked to be excused prayers and moves in a mysterious way' (*The Brand New Monty Python Book*). Is that the way you picture God? That if he does exist, he's ineffective and bears no relation to normal everyday life? At the best he is reserved for all the strange things that go on in a church building. Woody Allen in the film 'Love and Death' sums it up for many people, 'If it turns out there is a God, I don't believe that he is evil. The worst that can be said is that he is an under-achiever'.

We are left feeling that we just don't know what he is like. But what if you *could* know what he is like? If you could discover that he is alive and well and able to relate to you? Would you be interested? The God who is described in the wedding service is actually very different from the way he is often presented both by the media and, unfortunately, by the church as well. Many of our services suggest that God is unreal and couldn't, even if he wanted to, relate to us. We assume that he's like the service I used to attend: dull, boring and totally irrelevant. So what does the wedding service claim he's like?

Loving

The first words that are often used in the *ASB* service are a quotation from one of Jesus' closest friends. 'God is love and those who live in love live in God, and God lives in them' (1 John 4:16). Here is John, one of Jesus' disciples, trying to convey what this great and fantastic God is like, trying to sum him up. For John there is no religious jargon. He doesn't resort to the academic incomprehensibility of a university professor but just makes the most basic statement: 'God is love.' Nothing could be more simple or more profound. The best way to describe God is 'love'. It doesn't claim to say everything about him but it sums up what he is like.

So often God is portrayed as remote and cold, someone or something to fear. But John's description is that God is a person even though we cannot see him. You see, impersonal things cannot love. We all know that. They can *be* loved, but they cannot *show* love. We may love our car, computer, kitchen or jewellery but however well we treat them and look after them they are unable to reciprocate our love. We do not expect our car to suddenly have a crush on us or our cooker to start shaking when we walk in the room. But God has feelings and John says that they are for us. God is not against us or indifferent to us. God loves me, wants to be with me, to care for me and he's on my side. That's some claim!

God is relational

Love also suggests a relationship that is expressed by two parties. That is what we celebrate at the wedding. Two separate people come together to declare publicly their love for each other and to cement and develop that relationship. If God loves then he too must be relational. That means that it must be possible to know God and for him to get to know us. Otherwise, all this talk of love and God is totally meaningless. It offers the opportunity to experience God's love by entering into some kind of relationship with him. It must be possible for us to respond to his love for us.

God is strong
The danger is that we think of love only in terms of romance. Our idea of love is based on Mills and Boon and *Just 17* magazine. We wonder how God's knees can knock when he sees us. How can his heart flutter when we catch his attention? The apostle Paul sums up in the New Testament what kind of love it is that God has for us: 'But God demonstrates his own love for us in this, while we were still sinners Christ died for us.' God's love is not a romantic palpitation or cheap talk; it's a love shown in action: an action that cost his Son Jesus Christ his life on the cross. The Christian claim is that God sent his Son to die for us so that we could enter into a relationship of love with God himself. Love, the Bible writers claim, is the Son of God dying an awful death, to show how much he loved us.

Recently my children went away for a week. My older daughter, who is 4 years old, made me a heart. She carefully cut it out and crayoned it red. On the back in her best handwriting she wrote, 'I miss you daddy, love Jennifer.' She then posted it to me. Jesus on the cross is God's heart sent to each of us with a message 'I miss you, get in touch with me please.' Paul is saying God loves us, even though he knows that we may decide not to make the relationship with him. We may not want to take it any further, we may ignore him or even remove him but he still goes on loving us.

Most of us, if we are honest, love best when we are loved. We find it very hard to keep on loving when it is not returned. Unfortunately this happens from time to time in most human relationships. Yet God loves even when we do not return his love. It is not dependent on our reactions, our performance or our appreciation of him. His cost is costly, sacrificial and so, so strong. Yet it is open to us to experience it. But it is not meant to stop just with us as individuals. God intends his love to go on and transform our love for other people too, especially the person we may be about to marry. I think we would all want the love of a marriage to be sacrificial. To be willing to love beyond the limits of endurance, pressure and even pain. To love the other person even when they do not always act in ways that seem loving or when their attitudes are cold. We would want it to be costly. To go on loving when, even at times, little is given in return. To love, as the marriage service says, when health may diminish, when wealth may seem a long way off or times may just seem hard and bleak. We all want a love that will see us through those times. Not just a soppy romantic love, but a love that will keep us together, energise us and stir us into action. Our greatest wish would be for a strong love. One that seems unbreakable, that keeps going, that gets us through the hard times and adds to the joy of the good times. A love that we can depend on, a love that we can rely on, a love that we can trust with our whole hearts. Who wants to spend their lives checking up on love?

This is why God is so relevant. He intends that his love will not only change us but also transform the way we relate to others. God wants his love to impact our relationships and especially our marriage relationship. God wants us to share his love, to experience it in every aspect of our lives, to share it with others.

But you may be wondering how we know God is like that. Isn't it just my own wishful thinking or the fact that I have been brought up to think like that? People have even said to me 'You're a vicar and of course you're *paid* to say that!' There is a well-known saying that, if you want to know what your wife will be like when she gets older have a close look at your future mother-in-law. I'm not sure that this is always true but it is based on the simple fact that there is a close link between mother and daughter. The family likeness means that you can more fully understand one by studying the other. In the same way Christians claim that as you look at the person of Jesus – through the eyes of the contemporary witnesses, the Gospel writers – you can understand something of what God, his father, is like.

Many people carry a picture of their loved one around in their wallet or handbag. They rarely need much encouragement to get it out and extol the virtues of the one they love. The image does not convey everything about the person that they love but it tells us something. Jesus, God's Son, is described in the Bible as the image of the God we cannot see. The claim is that Jesus Christ was God's way of coming into our world in a way that we can understand. Surely there is no better way to help our understanding than God coming as a human being. We are reminded in the *ASB* service that 'Our Lord Jesus Christ himself was a guest at a wedding in Cana of Galilee.' If the Son of God went to a wedding, that may tell us something about what his presence at a wedding now might mean. It might give us clues about how that unseen guest might act at any wedding today.

One of Jesus' closest friends, John, provides an eye-witness account of the proceedings in his Gospel (John 2:1–11). He tells us that Jesus, his mother Mary and Jesus' followers, the disciples, were all invited to a wedding in the north of Israel.

Now weddings in Jesus' time were rather different from modern-day affairs. Life in general was a hard physical grind, so weddings gave an opportunity for celebrating and feasting. There was a lavish meal. Oxen and fat calves were killed and cooked. A procession of all the guests with singing, music and dancing would arrive at the place of the reception. Then love songs would be played and stories told as the celebrations continued.

I am sure that most couples look forward to their reception. Many have to book a venue a year or two in advance to get the place they want. But in Jesus' time you would have to make your booking for a week. That's one long blow-out! Poorer people would have to go to work in the day and return to the continuing celebrations in the evening. And the bill for all this was the groom's responsibility! It was vital to get this reception right for we have contemporary evidence of what happens when things went wrong. It was not unheard of for writs to be issued by the aggrieved relatives of the bride when food or drink ran out. This was why it was such a serious matter when the wine ran out at the reception attended by Jesus. It was socially embarrassing, legally dangerous and potentially catastrophic.

So how is John's historic account relevant to a wedding today?

Jesus was invited

It's a simple point but we notice that Jesus was invited to the wedding. As his mum was there, it's probable that family friends or relatives were getting married. They had asked Jesus to be one of the guests and to enjoy the celebrations. So is it possible that this unseen guest could be invited to attend a wedding now? This may seem a crazy idea even to consider. How can a historical figure be part of a wedding now? Yet he is more than just a figure of history. One of the central claims of the Christian faith is that Jesus, who came back from the dead, is still very much alive today.

So what does it mean to invite him and to have his presence in a real and meaningful manner? Now sending him an invitation might be a little tricky. How would you address it and where on earth (or even heaven!) would you send it? No, to invite him simply means to acknowledge that he is there and wants to be part of the wedding day and the marriage. It does not entail understanding everything about him, or being able to answer complex theological questions. It involves wanting to begin to say 'Yes' to the help he offers, however tentative that yes may be.

Anything to do with Jesus is often caricatured as boring and embarrassing, two features that no one would want at their wedding celebrations. Yet there was no problem with Jesus being invited to this wedding. He did not ruin everything. No one seemed to curl up with embarrassment. When talking to him people did not suddenly look at their shoes or make an excuse to leave. Conversation continued, laughing was much in evidence and everyone had fun. Jesus was not a killjoy or party-pooper! Quite the opposite. In fact, the religious people used to complain incessantly that Jesus spent too much time at parties and that he mixed with the party crowd rather than with them. All the religious types could not believe that he was both the Son of God *and* had fun. Yet he could and he did. The party crowd wanted to be with him and to spend time in his presence. Not just because he was the first religious person who had ever shown any interest in them, but he was so different from anyone that they had ever met before. Jesus did not act the way they expected him to. There were no moral lectures or putting people down. He just loved being with them and they in turn loved being with him.

He acted
Jesus did more than just turn up and join in the celebrations. His mum told him about the potentially embarrassing situation of the wine running out. Jesus then did something dramatic. In what John records as the first of his miracles, he changed some stone jars full of water into jars full of the best wine! The only people who were aware of what had happened were the catering staff and they knew, without any doubt, that he had acted. He had told them to fill six stone jars with water and then take it to the master of the banquet. They must have smirked and laughed as they saw all the guests sipping what had been just the local water and congratulating the groom on his choice of vintage wine!

Couples I meet often ask me how Jesus can make any difference in their lives or situation. The answer, I believe, is that as the living Son of God he is able to act today. He can act because, unlike us, he is not limited by his death. He returned from the dead, alive, never to die again. As the Son of God he is not limited to one place and to one time. His final promise to his friends was 'I will be with you to the end of the age', a promise which still stands.

Millions of people throughout history have claimed that he has acted and continues to act in their lives. Not only is he with them but he offers guidance, protection, care and help in the most practical of ways. He doesn't just sit around. The claim is that Jesus acts in the most nitty-gritty situations of married life. In giving patience when it is fast running out, in pouring in love when it's in short supply and in providing strength when it has been

WHERE DOES GOD FIT IN ON THE DAY?

spent. Through God's book, the Bible, Jesus also provides a framework for a couple's life together now and in the future. Jesus' amazing claim is that he puts all the infinite resources and qualities of the Living God at our disposal. That's quite some claim.

He provides the best

I received in the post this morning a special offer to join a motoring organisation that provides assistance when you break down. There were different levels of help that you could opt to purchase. Basically the more you were willing to spend the higher the level of service.

The good news is Jesus doesn't work like that. He offers us the top-level service at no charge and with no strings attached. When the wine ran out, he did not go and purchase a few bottles of cheap plonk, fetch a sample of his home brew or organise a quick whip-round. No, he changed about 180 gallons or over a thousand bottles of water into wine! And what wine it was. When the catering manager tasted it he congratulated the bridegroom for keeping the best wine for later on in the party, when most people would be less able to appreciate the difference! The bridegroom must have been wondering what on earth was going on. Where had all this wine been? He had not remembered ordering it and especially that much. But he must have!

In this extraordinary real-life tale we are reminded of Jesus' claim that he wants the best for us. He didn't just give a little help but he provided the best that anyone could want. His followers claim that he's just the same today. He provides the best for them. He himself said that he had come to bring life, and life in all its fulness (John 10:10). All too often the image portrayed by the church is that he came to bring dullness and life in all its blandness. Yet you have only to read his life-story to see that is patently false. Here was someone who lived life to the full and by his death and resurrection proved conclusively to his followers and to many others since that he could give life beyond the limits.

I sincerely believe Jesus wants married couples to have the best life, now and for ever. Though he is always there, he does wait for an invitation to be fully involved. He is patient and polite. He does not force his way in or force his presence upon us.

He went to extraordinary limits to make this offer of help. It is free but it is not a cheap offer. It cost Jesus his life on the cross. His death showed how far he would go. He wants us all to experience the best but it took all that he had to make that offer.

How can I ask him to act in our marriage?

In one sense this happens on the wedding day. It happens during the prayers which form an integral part of the service. I don't know what you think about prayer. Quite often it's the part of a church service when people think about lunch or what they are going to do in the afternoon. Some take the opportunity for a little snooze. Yet Christians claim that as we pray we open the gate to the eternal. In the words we utter, however mundane they may seem, the infinite and spiritual world touches our own earthly experience. It takes us up into God's presence, into the control room of the Universe. It also releases God's power and presence into our ordinary humdrum existence. It may all sound like something from a sci-fi novel and yet millions of Christians claim this a reality for them. A man soon to be married but with no formal religious attachment commented in a newspaper recently that the service 'Is a way of linking the present and eternity.' Understanding prayer like this helps to take away its association with school and boredom.

At weddings I see many reactions to the prayers that are either said by the minister, a friend or the whole congregation. Often understandably, it is the time to relax, giggle a bit, discuss the service so far. Yet if it takes us to God and brings his presence and power into our lives then it is an important part of the service. It is worth thinking about what prayers you want and your response to them on the day.

The prayers usually come after the vows and the sermon. The Lord's Prayer, which is that famous prayer that Jesus taught his closest followers and which most people still are able to remember from their school days, is often used at this juncture. The prayers can be led by the minister or suitable friends or relatives. If there are people who are able to do this, it can give the service that personal touch. Often the wedding service will contain some set prayers which can be used. Some churches will allow for those leading prayers to create their own. You should talk to your minister about this and find out what usually happens in his or her church. The prayers often ask for God's blessing on the couple, for his help as they set up a home, and for the upbringing of children, if that is to be part of the couple's plan. God is also asked to provide the resources for the couple to be the best partners that they can possibly be. Since Jesus shows us that God desires to act and provide the best for us, then these prayers are significant matters. They are not just idle religious jargon but meaningful requests for help and resources from a living and loving God.

Often prayers from the service books are used. For example, the *ASB* has about ten different possibilities, while the Roman Catholic service has three different groups of prayers, from which individual choices can be made. But you may also be able to find suitable prayers from other sources. You could ask your minister if he has anything that could be used. A visit to a local Christian bookshop might prove fruitful.

The prayers invite God to help the couple and to be a significant part of their day and lives. This often neglected area of the service is a vital ingredient of the whole day and of the couple's hopes for the rest of their lives together.

Through looking at the wedding service, we have asked God some questions about himself and his relationship to us. Hopefully this will give important information in considering how to treat the unseen guest. Will he stay a guest? Will he remain unseen? He would love not only to be there at the wedding, but to be involved in all that is happening. He wants to fit in by giving every couple all the resources he makes available. The question is: How much do they want to receive?

CHAPTER 4

What is happening to us at the wedding?

'MARRIAGE IS NOT A WORD it's a sentence' – King Vidor.

'You had better enjoy your last days of freedom' is often the dubious encouragement that couples approaching their wedding day receive. King Vidor's sentiments have become common currency. The liberty of singleness is lost and the restrictions of marriage are to be endured. Jokes are made about being 'under the thumb' or 'only being allowed out under licence!' Yet surely this marriage relationship has more to offer than a limit to freedom, enjoyment and pleasure. Does it really mean that the 'so-called fun and spontaneity of singleness' is to be given up for the drudgery of being tied down to one person? I don't think so!

Most married couples would strenuously deny such claims. Obviously their lives do not continue in exactly the same manner after they are married. Marriage implies change: change in the way a couple relate to each other and to those around them. There are bound to be things that each partner will want to change about the other's appearance, attitudes or actions. In a recent magazine article women voted for fifty changes they would make to their partner, including stopping him tucking his shirt into his underpants and drinking milk straight from the carton! But this new life together brings much to expect, desire and enjoy.

The opening section of the modern Anglican marriage service (*ASB*) reassures us of this as it explains the changes that happen as the couple are married before their families and friends and God. We have thought about how God fits in on this most special of days. We now need to consider how his presence affects the couple. At the beginning of the service, the minister reminds us that 'the scriptures teach us that marriage is a gift of God in creation'. This simply means that marriage is not an accident or a purely human convenience but is one of God's special inventions. The first book of the Bible, Genesis, records the beginning of civilisation and states that God intends a man and a woman to come together in an exclusive lifelong relationship. This necessarily entails a separation from their families and the forming of a new unit. God was not surprised by the fact that we are attracted to each other, that we want to be together and that we so strongly desire a shared intimacy. He made us to be like that. He does not look down in utter horror and surprise as couples get together. He is not a caricature of an austere and prudish Victorian father but a loving personal God who created us with relational and sexual desires. Billy Connolly ruefully commented that 'marriage is a wonderful invention but then again so is a bicycle repair kit'. As we look at what a wedding is all about I hope that you will see that his aside may over-inflate the importance of the repair kit!

As the couple stand at the front of the church it may be hard to imagine that this much is happening to them. Surely it's just the culmination of a legal contract. They become Mr and Mrs, but that's about it – now let's get on with the reception.

No, the service is fundamental, not only because it is a wonderful social and emotional occasion, but because it reminds us that marriage comes from the living God. This is why the service has such a deep significance.

The Anglican service goes on to state that 'marriage is a holy mystery in which man and woman become one flesh'. That may sound rather strange and creepy. Yet this notion of a couple becoming one flesh is the central idea about marriage in the whole of the Bible. When the Bible describes the life of the first human beings it comments that 'for this reason a man will leave his father and mother and be united to his wife and they will become one flesh' (Genesis 2:24). Jesus himself quoted the same words when discussing marriage, as did the apostle Paul.

What does it mean?

So what does it mean to become one flesh? It helps to know that when these words were written 'flesh' did not just imply the physical body. It suggests all the various aspects of our humanity, social and spiritual as well as physical. These words are trying to portray that God's gift of marriage produces a unity which is so close that it produces a oneness. The Methodist marriage service helpfully describes it as the lifelong union in body, mind and spirit. Put simply, two independent people are freely choosing to enter a relationship which is so deep and close that a wonderful oneness, unity and togetherness is created at the heart of their relationship.

If you have ever watched the best ice dancers, like Torvill and Dean, it sometimes seems that, despite being two individuals, they dance as one, in harmony and accord. The Bible is saying that the same thing happens in marriage when two individuals come together and begin to dance to the same tune. This does not mean an end to individuality, there is still a real distinctiveness. But there is a unity that cannot be achieved through other relationships. Marriage is much more than a friendship or casual liaison.

The depth of this union is illustrated by Jesus' words that are quoted towards the end of the service. 'So they are no longer two, but one for what God has joined together, let man not separate' (Matthew 19:6). This is the basis of the Christian idea that marriage is for life, a truth which flows from the unique oneness marriage engenders. It was not designed to be temporary or repeated.

These introductory words to the service go on to spell out how this union works out. This oneness does not depend simply on words spoken at a service but operates at all levels of this new relationship. It is a oneness physically, emotionally, socially and even spiritually. We humans are complex beings. We know that we are more than just physical entities who only need our physical appetites satisfied. We also have other desires which need to be met if we are to be fully human. I know very little about cars but I know that they are much more than just an engine. However big or good your engine is, an engine on its own is not a car. It is a most vital component without which you have no car. But it cannot work properly without wheels, chassis and all the other parts. To work as intended it needs all these other parts. As humans we are no different. We are not just one aspect but multi-dimensional. All the parts need to work together to fulfil our humanity and the relationship we were created for and yearn for.

A physical oneness

The most immediate expression of this oneness is the sexual aspect of the relationship. Sometimes it is felt that Christianity is ashamed of this part of our lives. Certainly some Christians have seemed to vindicate this view by their behaviour or attitudes. But according to the Bible this is not God's viewpoint. The Anglican service states that 'marriage . . . is given, that with delight in tenderness they may know each other in love and through the joy of the bodily union, may strengthen the union of their hearts and lives'. God is not against sex – it was his idea. But he also knows what a powerful force sex is and he wants to make sure it is used for our fulfilment. The sexual part of a relationship is vital in conveying the oneness of that relationship. The union of marriage is beautifully expressed in the physical union of husband and wife.

The danger of our sex-driven society is that this becomes the sum of our relationship. Yet we are much more than sexual beings. The physical aspect of any marriage relationship needs important consideration but it must not be divorced from the other aspects of the relationship. The service reminds the couple that the physical oneness will strengthen the union of their hearts and lives. It is not to be seen in isolation but recognised as part of God's plan to deepen a couple's love for each other. Sex often reflects the state of a relationship and also gives impetus to other areas of the couple's life together. The wedding service gives us an opportunity to get the physical aspect into its proper place and proportion. It affirms its importance in expressing a couple's oneness. But it also reminds us that this deep relationship has many other aspects that need to be thought about and lived out. In fact the physical union is a much more potent force when the other elements of the relationship have also been attended to. We are simply reminded that when all the parts work together, the sum is very powerful.

An emotional oneness

The word which is associated with weddings is 'love'. The introduction to the service reminds the couple and congregation that as 'husband and wife give themselves to each other in love throughout their lives, they shall be united in that love as Christ is united with his church'. The wedding is a proclamation of a unity in love. There is a reminder that this is not an automatic process. Though wedding and love are inextricably linked, one does not guarantee the other. The couple are reminded that they need actively to give themselves to each other in love. The emphasis here is on giving. To use the format of the famous cartoon series 'Love is . . . giving yourself to and for the other person.' It challenges us not to be selfish in our desire to *receive* love but to be selfless in *giving* love. It means not doing what we want when we want but putting the other first. This could be on the minor level of not immediately assuming that it will be all right if I watch my favourite TV programme. Or it might involve not making a major decision of life like suddenly deciding to move home, without first consulting and agreeing this with the other person. The words of the Anglican service go on to express what this practical love may mean, 'they may comfort and help each other, living faithfully together in need and in plenty, in sorrow and in joy'. It's a love which is emotional but also practical. A love which is guaranteed however the situations of life may vary. A love which is constant in good and not so good times. A love which is prepared to *keep on* loving and giving. This is what really unites a couple and gives their relationship the most sure and solid foundation. The service reminds us of the supreme example of giving love in Jesus. His love for his followers was so selfless that it led him to face death on a cross for them.

Such love will inevitably mean change. It is very difficult really to love someone while at the same time resolutely refusing to change. It will mean thinking about how they and their oneness can enable the other partner to become fully the person they want to be. Such a love allows the other person to develop to their fullest extent. For example it includes how the couple relate to each other. It affects what they do with their time and money, the kind of home they establish and their attitudes to a host of things. He won't be able to spend all his money on beer and cigarettes, and she won't be able to spend all hers on new clothes! A couple will need to think about what they want so that their values, lifestyle and actions reflect *both* their points of view. Above all, this needs good and constant communications. There must be a willingness to talk over things frankly, honestly and openly and, most importantly, a commitment to listen properly to your partner. It may mean being ready to change and admit you are wrong, something which isn't easy for any of us. Love is often misrepresented as purely an emotion that makes our hearts race faster, our palms sweat and our knees knock. Of course our emotions are part of love, but *only* part. This unity of love that the service describes is far deeper. It brings a couple together in a way that marks out this relationship from any other that is on offer.

Social oneness

The service also reminds everyone present that this unity relates not only to the couple themselves but also to everyone else. We are told in the Anglican service that 'they belong to one another and they begin a new life together in the community'. Social conditions have changed and a wedding does not necessarily mean two individuals leaving their family for the first time and starting up a new family unit together. Despite this, the wedding does create a new social institution. People will now look at the couple in a new way. A marriage is not just a quaint social custom or an outmoded convention. It allows a couple space in which to develop their oneness. They will need to work out how they relate to their family and friends. Obviously these old relationships are impor-

WHAT IS HAPPENING TO US AT THE WEDDING? 49

tant but marriage gives the couple a new focus and priority. The wedding service reminds them of their new prime relationship as the focus of their lives irrevocably shifts. This social oneness is easily ignored but is often the cause of many problems. Social oneness will change the way the couple relate to their families and friends. Not, of course, that these relationships end or are diminished but there is now a new centre for the couple's lives.

The couple need to work out how they are going to relate to their families and friends so that they neither ignore nor let them dominate their lives. Of course there are many mother-in-law jokes about their supposed interference. The couple need to make sure that they value their family's help and advice but without letting the family run their lives. Space and time are needed for this new unity to be worked out. It also needs support and help, and parents in particular need to be available without taking over. I heard recently of a mother-in-law who changed all the furniture round in a couple's home just after they had got married without being asked. She thought she was being helpful and creating more space for them! The wife was very upset though, as she thought her role in the new house was being usurped. It was the new couple's job to sort out their own life now. This is also true of friends. Old friendships are important and valuable but they must not be allowed to impinge on this new relationship. I sometimes meet husbands or wives who complain that their partners spend more time with their close friend than they do with them.

The other area of the so-called oneness that is mentioned in the Anglican service is the bringing up of children. In the older Anglican service (*BCP*), the role of bringing up children was given as the prime reason for marriage. In the new Anglican service this role is diminished to reflect the fact that this is not always the prime reason couples marry. Some couples do not wish to have children or unfortunately cannot have them. But for many couples this new unity may be experienced and expressed as they bring a new life into existence.

A oneness in faith

There is another part of the oneness which is often ignored or missed out. Its role in the relationship should be considered carefully. At the end of the long introductory section the minister says that 'we pray with them . . . that they may fulfil his purpose for the whole of their earthly life together'. God's purpose for our lives is more than a happy marriage, a prosperous career or a successful home. He desires above all that we will know him and then be used by him in his world. As a couple experience the wonderful unity of marriage, it may encourage them to think about and seek out the source of that unity. A wedding gives them an excellent opportunity to consider their relationship to God. It encourages them to think about the big issues of life. Why are we here? What is our future? Is there anyone beyond ourselves who can help us in our relationship? Is there anything beyond this life together? It is worth the couple talking together about their own beliefs – if only to see if their views may cause problems in the future. The wonderful thing is that as they discover a oneness with each other the possibility of their discovering a oneness with the living God opens up as well.

The secret of success

We all desire success. The heroes of our society are usually those who have made it in some way or another. Many books and videos offer a guide to success in everything from cooking or golf to sex and self-worth. As couples approach marriage they often want to know how to make it work. We are all aware of the present divorce rate and this only accentuates the desire for a success formula.

The service itself offers some advice. It simply reminds us that marriage is from God, and that it is a gift he gives to us for our benefit. Through this gift he transforms two individuals into a oneness that, while recognising their individuality, brings them together at the deepest levels of their existence. Sometimes in wedding services this union is symbolised by having two candles lit which represent the couple. These separate candles are used to light a central candle representing their new union and then the other two candles are extinguished. The danger in any marriage is that success is limited to one area. According to many magazines, performance in the bedroom is the essential element of any successful marriage. Others might think that love is the key to success or the production of children or how to cope with your relatives! The Bible's picture of becoming one flesh suggests that no one element is sufficient. We ignore any one of these aspects at our peril; each needs to be worked on and each part feeds the others. For example the physical element is improved when the emotional, social and spiritual parts are working well.

This may sound like hard work with little fun or enjoyment, yet it is not a life-sentence. No, as well as effort and application, there is much fun to be had working it out. And remember, God who gives us marriage also offers to help us as we work towards this true unity. The secret of success is to make the four parts of this unity work together. True unity in marriage is physical, emotional, social and spiritual, working in harmony.

CHAPTER 5

What do we promise?

THE MAIN ACTION in the wedding service comes, for most people, as the couple make the vows and promises to each other. These follow on from the minister's reminder about the possible legal impediments to marriage.

So what's so special about these words? Why are they so central to the whole service? Well, we know the importance of a promise. You have probably made at least one today. You may have left your house earnestly agreeing to be home by 6pm or you may have signed an agreement with your bank that, in return for their help in purchasing your new car, you will pay them back in 24 monthly instalments. Some promises are sealed by our words, others need a legal document to be signed.

So why do we make such promises? Why do we restrict ourselves in these ways? How come we take these responsibilities on? There seem to be three reasons why we are willing to commit ourselves in this manner.

First, what we are saying or doing is important enough to be marked out in a significant way. For example, in taking out a loan to buy a washing machine, I recognise that my promise to repay is significant. The bank would not be too pleased if, after a short time, I decided that I'd had enough. A promise reminds us that we are committed to certain actions and responsibilities. How many of us have been greeted with 'But you promised' on returning from a shopping trip without a certain item. I returned recently from a trip away without a toy that I said I would purchase. I was therefore welcomed by a screaming child who, knowing how to turn the screw, cried out, 'But Daddy, you said you would.' At that moment I could not have felt more guilty if I had held up a toy shop at gunpoint. There was no escape, no mitigating plea, and no immediate act of restitution. I had failed in a big way.

Second, the promise says something to the other person. You have now committed yourself to them through a particular action. It could be a verbal promise to a friend or a legal commitment to a mortgage lender. Whether it is a personal or business arrangement you are now, in some way, linked. The promise or agreement is to be fulfilled. You cannot just walk away when you feel like it. To fail might jeopardise a relationship or lead to a visit from the bailiffs.

Third, the promises act as a guide in their fulfilment. They're an aide-memoire to remind you of obligations undertaken. Quite often my promises return to haunt me. 'Are you going to start painting the spare room this weekend' my wife asked me the other day. This was a bit of a shock to me as I was planning a trip to a football match. 'Oh I don't think I can manage this weekend?' I replied lamely. 'Well why did you promise me last week to do it this weekend' she asked me in a manner that would have made Rumpole of the Bailey envious of her cross-examining ability. Game, set and match to Heather. The mists of my mind just at that moment revealed to me a flashback from last week. Unfortunately it reminded me of a rash promise to paint the aforementioned room. Sorry, but the football would have to wait. The contents of my words had to guide my actions if I was to retain my integrity. A promise is usually accompanied by conditions, guidance on its fulfilment and even a time limit. All these three elements of a promise apply to the wedding service. Now obviously such promises are in a different league from agreeing to bring back a 'take-away'. The wedding promises are some of the most profound promises anyone can make – but the same rules apply.

Of course, the promises at a wedding are not just decided upon there and then. In one sense the decision was made when the couple agreed to get married, whether that was a sudden event or discussed over time. The wedding service is not decision time about what to do but a public recognition of a decision which has already been made and a public commitment to each other and before God. This is highlighted in the introduction to the Roman Catholic service as the couple are reminded that on this their wedding day God seals and strengthens their love. I assume that as I ask a couple if they take each other as husband and wife they are not making up their mind there and then. I would be extremely concerned if there was a long pause while they said, 'I'll have to have a think about that.' The promises are a sign to seal their lifelong commitment to each other and an occasion to do so publicly and in God's presence. It commits them intimately to each other while reminding them of how to fulfil the promises and the responsibilities that will ensue.

This is exemplified by the first question the couple are asked by the minister, not only in the Anglican service but in most other Christian wedding services. They direct their answers of 'I will' to the minister, not to each other. In doing so they signify their willingness and freedom to marry. At this juncture in the service it's not a question of love or desire but a willingness to be married and to live out that married life. The order in the Roman Catholic service is slightly different as it splits this question into two parts around the promise that no legal impediment to marriage is known.

In the Anglican service, three elements of a promise are clearly seen in the words spoken by the minister to the couple. First, it is marked out as an important moment by the minister who reminds all present that this is done before God, each other and the congregation. Second, the link is made to a particular person. This is simply done by the names of each partner being used in the vows. The promise is not general but specific and exclusive. Finally, there is the reminder to those who make the promise of what this entails. This is not a casual arrangement or a hasty liaison. Each partner is reminded that the commitment involves love, comfort, honour and protection. The guidelines insist that all others will be forsaken and that faithfulness is now guaranteed.

The promises are permanent and exclusive. This is not the most popular feature of promises today. We tend to favour conditional agreements. 'I'll do this as long as . . .' or 'This only applies until . . .' In fact we are very cynical about total promises. Whenever we hear a politician categorically promising us something we look for the get-out clause, or we wait for him to say the next week that was not what he meant and he was taken totally out of context or misquoted! This malaise even affects weddings. We know that many celebrities make their promises already having made another promise about how they will split the money if the relationship crashes!

Now we all know that things do not work out as we wish and marriages do fail. But it is important not to approach the promises as temporary and therefore of diminished worth. These are not accessory agreements to be slipped in and out of or cast aside when they don't go easily. The *ASB* service moves rapidly on to the vows, the promises the bride and groom make to each other. As we discussed earlier this is marked by the couple turning to face each other while holding their partner's right hand. Most other denominations' vows are very similar to the Anglican churches with some minor exceptions. Many of them start with the additional phrase of 'I call upon these persons here present to witness that . . .'

The words they speak can be memorised, read or repeated after the minister. They are no longer addressed to the minister but to one another. Again the three elements of a promise are here. The significance of what they are doing is marked out in the *ASB* service by the reminder that 'This is according to God's holy law' and 'This is my solemn vow'. The solemn vow is a reminder that this promise has a power in law while the mention of God highlights the spiritual significance of this act. This spiritual aspect is not only because of the religious setting but because marriage is God's gift to people and the promises are made in the consciousness of his presence.

Second, the words of the promise say something to the other person. These words are not general statements of intent or a vague mapping out of a future course of action. They are intensely personal, relational and specific as they repeat 'I' then use their own name, 'take you' followed by their intended's name. This is not a memory jog of who they are marrying. You would hope they are aware of this information before this point in their lives. So why are names used? It highlights the personal commitment they are making to another while also reaffirming their own personal statement of intent.

The rest of the promise celebrates the wonderful responsibilities that follow on from their love and commitment to each other. It sets out the basis of the agreement they are making. Their commitment is all-encompassing, exclusive and intimate and is captured by the words 'to have and to hold'. This tries to sum up the Bible ideal of 'one flesh'. There is no suggestion of possession, subjugation or domination but of the deepest possible unity.

The words that follow, 'from this day forward' proclaim that all these promises begin now. It's not a future hope or something to grow into. The flag is down and the relationship has begun.

Next, the implications for the future of this present commitment are spelt out. This is not a casual or fair-weather contract which situation or circumstances will alter. Three particular examples are mentioned: for better or worse, richer or poorer and in sickness and in health. These promises are to be kept through all the varying conditions of our lives. We all know the temptation to go back on promises when the pressure is on. I might not stop off at the shops to pick up tea because I'd like to stay late to finish off all this work or I'm not sure finances will allow me to make my monthly payment. There are pressures too to overlook or ignore these marriage vows. As a couple get married everything is rosy and dream-like. There are no sightings of difficulties on the horizon, just guaranteed years of wedded bliss. Yet we all know life is not like that. Repeating these promises in church is not a magic incantation to ward off hard or difficult times. Many of the problems couples face are not even of their own doing but are purely the product of circumstances. We all face situations which may be far beyond our control. For example unemployment, serious illness or financial constraints, which can happen to anyone, put pressures on a marriage. But the marriage service makes it clear that these promises are not a conditional agreement that operates only as long as everything is running smoothly. There is no inbuilt marriage ejector seat which catapults us free from the relationship at the first sign of danger. The couple are asked to take the most difficult path of working through hard times because the relationship is of such immense worth. Mrs Antrobus sums up this attitude in Thomas Wilder's play 'Skin of the Teeth' when she says, 'I didn't marry you because you were perfect. I married you because you gave me a promise. That promise made up for your faults and the promise I gave you made up for mine. Two imperfect people got married and it was the promise that made the marriage.' The bottom line for any marriage is the commitment to keep true to the promises that have been made.

The basis of these promises, though, is not a cold financial or a calculated contractual agreement. It is based on that agreement 'to love and cherish'. These attitudes are the foundation upon which everything else is built. To cherish simply means to value someone or to hold them dear. It means treating the other person as they deserve to be treated, and to value them for all they are.

Think about what you value most in your house. It may be a painting, ornament, cup, medal, plant or something else. How do you rate it? Would you forget about it, lose it or put it out of the way? No, probably you would enjoy it, take care of it and even give it pride of place. Now if that's how we treat our most treasured things how much more should we take care of, enjoy and love our partner. It is worth a couple considering how they can show their appreciation to each other daily by words and actions. It may not always be easy with so many pressures upon us and time at a premium.

To obey or not to obey?

In the modern Anglican service (*ASB*) the service offers the couple a choice of words at this juncture. They can either decide that both parties will promise to love and cherish or the alternative is that the groom promises to love, cherish and worship while the bride loves, cherishes and obeys. In the older service (*BCP*) there is no choice. The groom promises to love and cherish while the bride loves, cherishes and obeys. The minister will usually talk to the couple about their preference. It is worth them spending a little time thinking about this issue. (Not all services offer a choice and some include obey, while others do not.) It is worth looking at the service you will be using to discover what it offers.

This whole issue may seem rather pedantic. Does the use or non-use of one word really matter? The truth is that sometimes it does mean a lot to one or both of the partners. I was talking to a bride-to-be recently who very firmly told me that there was no way she would ever say the word 'obey' to her partner. I asked her why she felt so strongly about this issue. In her reply it was obvious that the use of this word carried with it connotations of subjugation and blind obedience. 'It means he can call all the shots and I've just got to accept it' she told me. 'We want an equal relationship with joint responsibility, not a boss and slave' she added. Yet is this the function the word has in these promises? What does the ceremony mean when it chooses to use the word 'obey'?

The origin of the promises in their present form goes back to the Middle Ages but a direct link can be traced right back to the Bible. Paul in his letter to the church in Ephesus instructs 'wives to submit to their husbands as to the Lord' (Ephesians 5:22). Before anyone thinks this is typical male domination it is worth taking note of the preceding verse which instructs everyone, male and female to 'submit to one another'.

So the basis for this obedience is not just one-sided. Its starting point is everyone's attitude to everybody else. The danger is that in the twentieth century we link obedience or submission with power and domination. But in the Bible submission or obedience is about attitudes not our rights. The attitude is a desire to be selfless and not to press always for our own way. It is not a declaration that I am now a second-class citizen who abrogates all rights. It certainly does not give the partner carte blanche to command, 'Whatever I say goes.' It's definitely not the obedience demanded by a sergeant major, a teacher or your boss at work. How can such a form of obedience ever be integrated with the joint promises to love and cherish? No, it suggests a willingness to accept the other's wishes not out of subjection but willingly, because of love.

For the church, the supreme example of such obedience is Jesus himself. In another letter Paul wrote, he suggested we should share Jesus' attitude. He was God in human form but because of his love for us he willingly entered into our frail flesh even to the point of death. His life illustrates the right attitudes of obedience, love and self-giving that are required in a marriage.

When a bride claims that she struggles with the promise to obey, I often wonder whether the groom realises that, according to the Bible, his response to his wife's submission is 'love your wives, just as Christ loved the church and gave himself up for her' (Ephesians 5:25). What a love husbands are asked to demonstrate! This is the love that compelled Jesus to give up his own life voluntarily for his followers. Surely to give up your life for someone else is proof of a total and ultimate love. Now I am not suggesting that Paul is hinting that a groom should go *that* far for his bride! But he is saying that's the *kind* of giving, self-sacrificing and unconditional love you should be looking to offer. This is summed up in the service by the use of the word 'worship'. We often talk about 'worshipping the ground she walks on' to sum up someone's devotion. That's some tall order isn't it? It means giving total respect and honour and going to any lengths for them. It's not just the bride who has to make big promises. The groom is not to take advantage of his wife's loving obedience. His response is quite the opposite. It is a response of total devotion and adoration.

As a couple think about this choice of words, I would urge them to consider the meaning of the words they will be saying. Do they convey what the couple want to say about their attitudes to each other? In some denominations there is a greater flexibility over choice of words and they may even, with certain guidelines, be able to write their own vows. Ultimately the choice is theirs. They must feel comfortable with what they are saying and that it expresses their sentiments.

After the vows, in whatever form they have been made, the next part of the service is the cue for the best man's heart to race. This is the moment for the exchange of rings. The modern service (*ASB*) offers a choice over the number of rings, as do most other denominational services. A couple can either receive a ring each or alternatively just the bride. In the older service (*BCP*) the service only allows for the bride to receive a ring from her partner, though most churches allow two to be used if the couple so wish.

The minister asks the best man (or woman) for the rings and then in the *ASB* service says a short prayer. The prayer is a statement of the significance of this act. It states that the rings are not just a quaint custom or an exquisite piece of jewellery. The ring has two functions. First, it is a symbol and second, it acts as a reminder.

The circular shape of the ring, with no beginning or end is symbolic of the couple's love and commitment. A ring (usually) is unending with no natural break so it symbolises 'unending love and faithfulness'. This love and the promises made are for ever. Its second function is to act as a reminder of the promises made. As I write this, my wife has gone to visit her parents for a few days. But just because I will not see her today does not end our marriage. To help me remember that, the gold ring I can see on my finger as I work is a clear reminder to me that we are married – if I needed reminding of that wonderful fact.

The ring acts as a statement to the couple and everybody else that they are married and that respect should therefore be paid to that exclusive partnership. It is an outward sign of the significance of their wedding day. The ring is a glorious reminder of promises made and a gentle warning to others that the love promised is now exclusive to one person. It serves to encourage us to keep on loving and to direct that love only to one person.

The service continues with the groom placing the ring on the bride's finger. If two rings are used this is followed by the bride doing the same for the groom. As they perform this action they will repeat certain words. The precise form differs in most of the services at this point but they all remind the couple that the ring is a sign of their marriage. The remainder of the words highlight the giving nature of their promises, a giving which is both physical and emotional. Their mode of acting towards the other is stressed with the words in the *ASB* service 'With my body I honour you.' The older service (*BCP*) substitutes the word 'worship' rather than 'honour'. Then they promise to offer everything to the other and to share all they have. These words affirm that selfless giving is essential to any marriage. There is no place for holding back or keeping what is perceived to be mine. The old independent life is lovingly given up to a new relationship which is to be shared and enjoyed together. If two rings are exchanged both partners say the same words. There is no differentiation of what they give up or what they put into this relationship. It is not usually very easy to give up so much. Yet this selfless love compels them to share themselves and all they have. This is not a forced act. It is not 'You must' but 'I want to'. Love does this. It transforms us from selfish to selfless, and from grasping to giving.

This may all seem to ask a lot from a couple who make these promises. How can anyone love like this? Surely this is far too demanding and idealistic? Are not the expectations far too high? Won't they only lead to disappointment? Well, the last words in the vows give us a clue to how a couple can live out what they have promised as they state this is all done 'within the love of God'.

These promises are indeed far-reaching and require a lot of us but God, who is the source of all love, has the resources available to help us. This was never meant to be a 'go it alone' venture. God has given us marriage and he offers us the possibility of living it out with him, strengthened by his love and power.

After the promises have been made the couple can relax as the minister takes over. He proclaims to everyone present what they have done. Again, most other churches follow a similar pattern at this point to the *ASB* service.

First, the minister reminds the audience that God has been present throughout the service. This has all been completed in his presence as well, of course, as family and friends. Then the minister simply repeats what the couple have committed themselves to, as he summarises this love contract. Their declaration of commitment has been accompanied by certain actions and because of all this they are now husband and wife. The minister joins their right hands and quotes Jesus' words, 'What God has joined let no man divide' (Matthew 19:6).

Again we are faced with the reality that this is not purely a legal contract but an agreement of spiritual significance as the inventor of marriage unites a couple. God's presence both encourages the couple and warns all others to respect and support God's work.

The couple usually kneel at this point and the minister prays for God's blessing on them. A blessing is simply asking God to make his resources and help available to them in real and practical ways.

Although the service has not yet ended the couple are now married before God and in law. This is often the moment when the minister tells the groom that he may now kiss his bride. There are other parts of the service to complete and registers to sign but the promises have been made. This is the most important contract either person will ever make. There is excitement as they look to the future but also a realisation of the seriousness and depth of the occasion. For these promises are not made to a faceless person in your life. This is the one you will love, cherish and even worship. The promises remind us that in marriage there is much to be gained from a partner but also everything to give.

Behind all these words, promises and actions is a faint echo. It serves to call our attention to the fact that in living this way, in selfless love and giving, however imperfectly, we are weakly reflecting the love God has for us. Our love will never match God's but even in its weakness it points us to that greater love.

That love, as revealed to us through the life of Jesus, is set before us not only as our supreme example but also as something freely available to us now, to help us live out the loving promises that have been made.

CHAPTER 6

Is that the end, or just the beginning?

'IT ALL HAPPENED SO QUICKLY, it was like a flash' Sally commented to me when we met a few weeks after her wedding. 'There was so much preparation in getting ready for the big day and then it was over.' Many couples feel this way after the service and day. There is so much to do. There is the service itself, before which a couple may meet with the minister to talk both about the wedding itself and issues related to marriage. (In many churches such an evening or course is offered to to a couple to prepare them for the day and marriage. It is well worth attending. It may be run by the minister, members of the congregation or both.) Hymns need to be chosen as you decide what your relatives and friends might know and what is appropriate to the day. You may be asked whether you have a Bible reading you would like at the service or if there is anyone who might lead the prayers. If you are producing your own service sheets these need to be agreed in advance with the minister and then prepared and printed.

But this is not the end of the preparations. I know from my own wedding that the organisation mushrooms. There may be ushers to be chosen and prepared for duty, buttonholes to be made and allocated. Recently I came into church to find the groom and best man in total panic as all the buttonholes had been left behind. 'Would there be enough time to go and get them?' they asked me in desperation. Eventually the buttonholes arrived with the bride! While a few photographs were taken of her they were quickly passed around to the requisite lapels! There are decisions to be made about what the bridesmaids, best man and ushers will wear.

The rings need to be bought and then passed safely on to the best man, who we all hope will remember them on the day. Cars have to be booked to get the bride and her attendants to the church and a photographer found whose pictures will not look as if they have been taken with a cheap pocket camera. The couple will have to decide if they want the ceremony videoed and discover whether this is acceptable to the minister and the church.

All this, and then there's bound to be something or someone who has been left out of the calculations. Suddenly at the church it's realised that Great Aunt Ethel, who you promised to organise a lift for, must be sitting at home waiting for someone . . . Aaagh! At least you will not have to organise a wedding like one I read about today in the paper. Held in India, it was attended by 150,000 people. The guests ate in shifts of 20,000 and the tables covered nearly thirty acres. The ceremony was decorated with twenty truck-loads of flowers. Imagine planning all that!

Yet even with all this detailed planning, which turns the simple coming together of a man and a women into something like a full-scale military operation, the service is quickly over. The event hopefully is a success, the planning worthwhile and the mission is accomplished: they are husband and wife. They leave the church together to start their new life. Outside the building they have to contend with the demands of the photographer before going on to enjoy the wedding reception and their new life together.

My hope is that even though the service may be over in what seems like a flash, their leaving the church will not be the end of their association with it. This need not be the end but just the beginning of finding out more about Jesus Christ.

There is no need for the couple to feel that any search for spiritual significance has now to come to a halt. The church will not be shutting the door on them. Hopefully the service and its preparation will have given the couple a positive view of the church. Many people's preconceptions of the Christian faith are challenged by their experience of the service. They discover that the ministers are not strange, other-worldly figures but ordinary people with a desire to serve and communicate Jesus Christ. The Christian faith is not boring and irrelevant but exciting and related to every area of our lives. Above all, God is not a remote, powerless entity but a real living and loving person who wants to meet with us on an individual level.

So if a couple want to come back, what can they do? They may feel embarrassed about returning, or not sure how to discover more. They may have more questions than answers and not even be sure what they are looking for. So here are three suggestions for positive action.

1. Come back to the church

They've gone out as they left the wedding service but they can come back. They will receive the most warm welcome. A church is the best place to meet with God, in the company of others who also want to meet with him. Of course you do not have to go to church to relate to God but it certainly makes it much easier. They will have the big advantage of already knowing the minister and maybe some of the congregation. The quicker they return after the wedding the easier will be that initial step back into the church. If you are recently married don't leave it too long or say 'We will settle down first' because the likelihood is that you will find it much harder further down the track. If God has so much to offer you and your relationship, it's worth finding out what difference he can make now.

2. Pray

This may seem a radical suggestion but it's the best way of getting to know God. You don't need to do anything religious to communicate with him. All you have to do is to talk, whether audibly or in your head. Tell God how you are feeling, thank him for his presence and ask him to help in specific ways. There's no need to try and pray for a long time, a minute is better than nothing. Pray when you wake up or go to bed or when you lose your temper or patience. Remember God wants to be involved in the most practical ways.

A couple may have been given a Bible or gospel at their wedding. They can read about the life of Jesus in one of the four gospels, Matthew, Mark, Luke or John. They could read a little each day and they will discover more about the most amazing person who ever walked on this earth.

3. Find out more

So often we base our decisions about the Christian faith on what we learnt at school and what we hear from other people. We reject it without really knowing why, except to say it's not for us. But what *is* it about? What lies behind the estimates that 59,000 people each day in this world start to follow Jesus? It's worth considering. Many churches run informal groups or discussions to help people discover the truth for themselves. These groups don't try to impose views or tell people what to believe but they do offer the opportunity and space to explore a little bit more in a safe environment. It might be helpful to ask if your church runs or knows of such a group .

Alternatively, there are many books available that simply and clearly explain the Christian faith and why it's credible. A minister will be able to point people to some helpful reading or your local Christian bookshop. Three suggestions for a place to start are *Why Bother With Jesus?* by Michael Green (Hodder), *It Makes Sense* by Steve Gaukroger (S.U.) or *My Life* by the comedian Bobby Ball (Spire) which tells how he found Jesus for himself.

'Now' is always the best time to do something. Not a few weeks later, or when a couple are established or when they have the time. The danger is that we just don't get around to it. The wedding service has one powerful message to all of us: the God of love wants to meet with us. He met with the couple as they were married but he doesn't want it to be a one-off get together. Just as there is scope for the couple's relationship to develop, so too it's possible to develop a relationship with God. We can, if we wish, close the door on him as we leave the church. Or we can leave it open to explore more and to enter, however tentatively. Whatever happens. I can assure a couple that God waits for them with unfailing and total love and care, and immense patience.

These words found in the last book of the Bible sum up God's attitude to us. They remind us that if we want God in our lives he will not disappoint. If we respond to him he will act. They are God's promise to each of us 'Here I am! I stand at the door and knock. If anyone hears my voice and opens the door, I will come in' (Revelation 3:20).

A newly married couple don't have to go out of the church and stay out; God himself invites them to come back in. I hope they will respond to him.

APPENDIX 1

Suggested readings

John 15:9–12
Jesus tells his friends to know his love so that they can love others.

Ephesians 3:14–21
This is a prayer for Christ's presence in the lives of the Christians which focuses on the request that they will realise his great love for them.

Ephesians 5:21–33
The Apostle Paul describes how a husband and wife are to be responsible for and to each other and how their attitudes should mirror Jesus' love for his people, the church.

1 Corinthians 13
A reminder to a church full of division that the most important quality we can ever possess is love.

Matthew 7:24–7
Jesus' vivid story about the choice we all face of what we are going to base our lives upon.

Colossians 3:12–17
The apostle Paul describes qualities and resources which God wants to make available to us.

1 John 4:7–21
John tells us that God is the source of all human love. He then describes what our practical response to that love should be like.

John 2:1–11
An eye-witness account of Jesus at a wedding where he has the most amazing influence and saves a most embarrassing situation.

APPENDIX 2

Popular wedding hymns

THIS IS NOT an exhaustive list of all the wedding hymns that are available. The church minister will be able to show you the hymn books the church has available This does not necessarily limit your choice as you could have the words of a hymn printed out on an Order of Service. If you are not sure about what to choose, the minister will be able to give useful advice. Remember to think about what those coming to the service will know as they have to sing the hymns. It is also important to look at the words of the hymns to make sure that they express what you want to say on such an important occasion.

The following hymns are a selection of well-known and popular wedding hymns. Look them up in a hymn book and see if they might be suitable for you.

All creatures of our God and King
All people that on earth do dwell
All things bright and beautiful
At the name of Jesus every knee shall bow
Blessed assurance, Jesus is mine
Christ is made the sure foundation
Come down O love divine
Crown him with many crowns
Dear Lord and Father of mankind
Great is thy faithfulness
Guide me O thou great Jehovah

Give me joy in my heart
Hallelujah sing to Jesus
I cannot tell why he, whom angels worship
Immortal invisible, God only wise
Jesus is Lord! Creation's voice proclaims it
Lead us heavenly Father
Lord Jesus Christ, you have come to us
Lord of all hopefulness
Lord, for the years, your love has kept and guided
Love divine, all loves excelling
Morning has broken
New every morning is the love
Now thank we all our God
O for a heart to praise my God
O God beyond all praising (Tune: I vow to thee)
O Jesus I have promised
O worship the King
Praise my soul, the King of heaven
Praise to the Lord, the Almighty, the king of creation
Rejoice, the Lord is King
Shine, Jesus shine
The Lord's my shepherd
This is the day

APPENDIX 3

Any questions?

THE ANSWERS GIVEN HERE set out broad guidelines but must not be regarded as definitive statements of the law. You should talk through any specific areas of uncertainty with your minister as soon as possible. Please note that these guidelines refer primarily to the practice of the Anglican Church in England and may not necessarily apply to other church denominations or in other parts of the United Kingdom.

1. Do I need to be baptised in order to get married in a Church of England church?

Basically, no. Every resident in the geographical area known as a 'parish' is entitled by law to be married in the church of that parish, unless (a) they are divorced and their former spouse is still alive (see Question 6) or (b) they are related to their proposed partner by one of the categories for which marriage is prohibited (see Question 12) or (c) they are under age (see Question 13). However, this right to be married in church without having been baptised only applies where the marriage takes place after banns have been published (see Question 3). If you wish or need to be married by common or special licence (see Questions 2 and 3), the bishops are under no obligation to issue such a licence if one or both parties are unbaptised. However, they may dispense with this requirement and allow ministers to exercise their discretion in individual cases.

2 Can we get married in the pretty church in the next town?

Only in exceptional circumstances. In order to be married in a particular church, at least one of you must live in the parish or be on the parish's electoral roll (i.e. be a full member of that church). Subject to the agreement of the ministers in both the parish where you live and the parish where you want to get married, it may be possible to obtain a special licence from the Archbishop of Canterbury's office. However, these are only granted in exceptional circumstances, such as where there has been a strong personal or family connection with the parish in the past and not simply because the church has a pretty setting.

3. What are banns and do we need them?

Banns are the main way in which (a) you formally declare your intention to marry and (b) it is established publicly that you are legally entitled to do so. Banns are published (i.e. read out) at the main (usually morning) service on three Sundays prior to the wedding. Those with a valid objection to your getting married are thereby given the opportunity to say so! You do not have to be present when your banns are published though you would of course be very welcome. The marriage must take place within three months of the banns being published for the third time. If the wedding is delayed beyond three months for any reason, the whole process must be repeated. Provided you give the required notice, fill in the form correctly and pay the relevant fee, you are entitled to have your banns published in the church of the parish where you live, even if, on other grounds (e.g. if one of you is divorced) the minister would not solemnise the marriage himself (see Question 7). Under certain circumstances (e.g. if one partner is a national of a country outside the old Commonwealth, European Union or United States), banns are not suitable and a common licence should be obtained instead. Your minister will tell you how to go about applying for this. Banns are not published when a marriage is to take place by licence.

4. Where do banns need to be published?

If you both live in the parish where the wedding is to take place, banns need only be published there. But if either of you lives in another parish, banns need to be published there as well. If you both live outside the parish and are exercising the right to marry in the church where one or both of you are on the electoral roll, banns need to be published in that church and the churches of the parish or parishes where each of you lives. The ministers of the other church or churches will give you a certificate to pass on to the minister who is conducting the wedding.

5. How can we get married in our parents' church if we've moved away?

To marry in a parish church after banns, you must actually live in the parish. It is possible, however, to obtain a common licence on the strength of a parish being your 'usual place of residence' for fifteen days before the licence is granted. Alternatively, you can apply for a special licence (see Question 2).

6. What happens if, after booking the wedding, we move house before it's due to take place?

Tell the minister as soon as possible as it may be necessary to apply for a licence rather than marrying after banns.

7. One of us has been divorced. Can we get married in church?

The law permits the remarriage of a divorced person in church when a former spouse is still living. However, it also allows ministers the freedom not to officiate at such marriages or allow their churches to be used. Some exercise that freedom and refuse to remarry divorcees under any circumstances. Others are more flexible but may need to know about the circumstances leading up to the divorce. The local bishop may be involved in this process.

An alternative service, called 'A Service of Prayer and Dedication after Civil Marriage', is available for couples who, although unable actually to marry in church, would nevertheless like to commit their relationship formally to God. Ask your minister for details.

8. How much will it cost?

Church of England fees for the publication of banns and the marriage service are standard and fixed by Parliament each year. You will also have to pay for extras like the organist, choir and bell ringers, together with the costs of heating and lighting. Compared with what the rest of the day usually costs, the charges for the church service are relatively small.

9. Can we be married in church if we have been living together?

As stated in answer to Question 1, the law gives all residents the right to marry in their parish church. There are certain exceptions but living together is not one of them. If, as sometimes happens, a minister declines to conduct the ceremony himself, it is his responsibility to find an alternative minister.

10. Who can act as witness in signing the register?

Anyone over 18, whether or not they are related to you. It's up to you to decide.

11. Can we get married at any time?

The timing of the service should be arranged with the minister. In any event, a marriage service must take place between 8am and 6pm (unless some other time is permitted by a special licence, something which is only done in cases of extreme medical necessity).

12. Who are the relatives that a person may not marry?

You may not marry a parent, child, adopted child, grandparent, grandchild, brother or sister, aunt or uncle, niece or nephew. Providing that certain safeguards are observed, it is now possible to marry a step-child, step-parent, step-grandparent or former spouse's grandchild. Such marriages may not take place after banns but only by licence.

13. How old must we be to marry?

You may not marry if either partner is under 16 years of age. If either partner is over 16 but under 18 years of age, the marriage may take place as long as no objection is raised by a parent or guardian when banns are published.

14. What happens if we want the service to be conducted by a minister who is not part of the parish?

Anglican ministers may usually do this, provided that the local minister agrees. Under certain circumstances, the bishop's approval will also be required. Anglican ministers who were ordained outside the British Isles must have the permission of the Archbishop to exercise ministry in England.

Ministers (or lay people) of other denominations may assist but they may not solemnise the marriage itself.